This Fragile Planet

His Holiness The Dalai Lama *on* Environment

Photography & text compiled & edited by Michael Buckley

"It is not difficult to forgive destruction in the past that resulted from ignorance. Today, however, we have access to more information, and it is essential that we re-examine ethically what we have inherited, what we are responsible for, and what we will pass on to coming generations."

"My hope and wish is that one day, formal education will pay attention to what I call education of the heart. I look forward to a day when children and students will be more aware of their emotions and feel a greater sense of responsibility both towards themselves and towards the wider world. Wouldn't that be wonderful?"

Cover Photo:
His Holiness arrives for teaching at the Tsuglagkhang, Dharmsala. **Photo: Michael Buckley**

Previous Page:
Dawn in Tibet — Panoramic sweep of high peaks, from Makalu and Chomolonzo (at left) to Everest, Khama Valley (at right). **Photo: Colin Monteath**

Left:
LTWA graphic depicting the four Tibetan Elements — Earth, Water, Fire and Air. Space is the 5th element.

Contents

Introduction	7
Moral Compass	11
Sacred Landscape	23
Preserving the Third Pole	51
Asia's Lifeline	69
Thinking Globally	87
Call to Action *HH Dalai Lama's Gift*	99
Parting Shots *Environmental solutions from the Tibetan World*	110
References & Resources	116

Introduction
by Michael Buckley, project editor

Left:
His Holiness looks out across Nubra Valley, north of Leh, Ladakh.
Photo: Tenzin Choejor

With the widespread impact of COVID-19 raging through 2020 and 2021, this has become a fragile planet indeed. Entire nations have come to a standstill — with flights grounded, livelihoods disrupted, and health-care workers under siege. The nation of India has witnessed millions of cases of the coronavirus.

This Fragile Planet actually derives from a quote from His Holiness appearing toward the back of this book. And while he refers to the planet in general, he often cites Tibet's ecology as being fragile — due to its special high-altitude ecosystems which, once damaged, take a very long time to recover.

This book focuses on His Holiness the Dalai Lama's commitment to environmental preservation, pairing quotes with inspirational imagery from more than a dozen professional photographers. His Holiness the Dalai Lama needs no introduction as a spiritual icon — and beacon. Lesser known is his lifelong commitment to environmental protection. It was largely on this basis that he was awarded the Nobel Peace Prize in 1989 — for his global initiatives for peace, human rights, and for preserving the environment. This was, in fact, the first Nobel Peace Prize ever awarded for an environmental initiative. His Holiness proposed a five-point peace plan to set aside Tibet as a zone of peace and a sanctuary for the environment. He proposed transforming Tibet into the world's largest natural park or biosphere, with strict laws to protect wildlife and plant life, careful regulation of natural resources, and a policy of sustainable development in populated areas. He envisioned Tibet as "a sanctuary of peace in the strategic heart of Asia."

What can the ancient faith of Tibetan Buddhism contribute to solving the climate crisis, the most urgent issue of our time? A lot, as it happens.

Tibetan Buddhism promotes a spiritual connection to the earth, embracing belief in sacred landscape: sacred peaks, valleys, lakes and rivers to be left totally untouched — to avoid angering resident guardian deities and spirits. In a sense, Tibetans created the world's first national parks, although not called by that name. These

realms were sanctuaries set aside by High Lamas. These initiatives date back to the 15th century, far in advance of similar concepts in the West. By asking for all of Tibet to be set aside as a sanctuary between China and India, His Holiness the Dalai Lama continues this tradition in more pressing times.

When it comes to nature, Tibet is a land of superlatives. The photography in this book aims to showcase the delicate ecosystems of Tibet, with the highest peaks and the deepest gorges on the planet. Unfortunately, these high-altitude ecosystems are under serious siege. Outside of the Arctic and Antarctic, Tibet has the world's largest store of ice and snow and permafrost, leading to its designation as 'The Third Pole.' The glaciers are rapidly melting, due to climate chaos factors. Since 1950, under Chinese rule, Tibet's forests and wildlife have been decimated, the land scarred by rampant mining, and the rivers wrecked by megadams — all of which have great impact on the nations downstream, particularly on the mighty rivers that are sourced in Tibet and flow across Asia to empty into the sea.

Considering Tibet's ecological significance to the world, it is alarming that the region is absent from global climate discussions. The global fight against climate chaos cannot be won without saving Tibet's unique and fragile environment.

Climate emergency is the most daunting issue facing humans today. Addressing lack of action concerning climate change, American scientist Gus Speth puts it in a nutshell: "I used to think the top environmental problems were biodiversity loss, ecosystem collapse and climate change. I thought that with 30 years of good science we could address those problems. But I was wrong. The top environmental problems are selfishness, greed and apathy … and to deal with those we need a spiritual and cultural transformation … and we scientists don't know how to do that."

From the Buddhist perspective, environmental degradation is the result of our ignorance, selfishness, greed, and lack of respect for nature. Tibetan Buddhism can deal with that, because it has developed a system of ethics and beliefs that respect and protect nature, embracing compassion for all sentient beings — and stressing how all life is interconnected. That is precisely what His Holiness the Dalai Lama brings to the table: advocating spiritual transformation and secular ethics, promoting universal responsibility, and fostering great respect for nature.

Right:
Peak in Yading Nature Reserve, Sichuan.
Photo: Michael Buckley

> "My third commitment is the issue of Tibet. This includes working to protect the Tibetan environment, as well as the identity and well-being of the Tibetan people, and preserving Tibetan culture and freedom of religion."

The Dalai Lama's Four Commitments

HH Dalai Lama has cited four principal life-long commitments to honour. The first is to promote peace and happiness, fostering human values such as compassion, forgiveness and tolerance — what he refers to as 'secular ethics.' The second commitment is to find ways to promote religious harmony and understanding among the major religious traditions of the world. The third commitment is to foster the preservation of Tibet's natural environment and the preservation of Tibetan culture. And the fourth commitment is about reviving the Nalanda tradition, and spreading awareness of ancient Indian knowledge.

> "Regarding Tibet's political matters, I have already retired. But regarding Tibet's ecology and very rich culture, I'm fully committed. We human beings have these marvelous, brilliant minds. But we are also the biggest troublemakers on the planet. Now we should utilize our brains with compassion, and a sense of concern. This is why one of my commitments is promotion of deeper human values."

Moral Compass

" Destruction of nature and natural resources results from ignorance, greed and lack of respect for the earth's living things… *"*

*Message from His Holiness
on World Environment Day,
June 5, 1986*

> Under a tree was the great Sage Buddha born
> Under a tree, he overcame passion
> And attained enlightenment
> Under two trees did he pass in Nirvana
> Verily, the Buddha held the tree in great esteem.

Poem from The Sheltering Tree of Interdependence, *composed of 30 stanzas by HH Dalai Lama, published in 1993 in Tibetan, along with an English translation. The poem was written to mark the opening in New Delhi of the International Conference on Ecological Responsibility: A Dialogue with Buddhism.*

Left:
His Holiness under the sacred Bodhi Tree, Bodhgaya, India, where the Buddha is said to have attained enlightenment.
Photo: Manuel Bauer

Right:
Fresco of Dalai Lama XIV with Nobel Peace Prize symbolised by white dove, painted on wall at Norbulingka Institute, Dharamsala, India.

Opposite:
The majestic sacred peak of Kawakarpo, in east Tibet (present-day upper Yunnan).

"Today's challenges are so great — and the dangers of misuse of technology so global, entailing a potential catastrophe for all humankind — that I feel we need a moral compass we can use collectively without getting bogged down in doctrinal differences. One key factor that we need is a holistic and integrated outlook at the level of human society that recognizes the fundamentally interconnected nature of all living beings and their environment. Such a moral compass must entail preserving our human sensitivity and will depend on us constantly bearing in mind our fundamental human values. We must be willing to be revolted when science — or for that matter any human activity — crosses the line of human decency, and we must fight to retain the sensitivity that is otherwise so easily eroded."

— *The Universe in a Single Atom*

" Since I too have a responsibility in this matter, (i.e., to work for the protection of the environment and to see that the present and future generations of mankind can make use of refreshing shade and fruits of trees), I bought these seeds of fruit-bearing trees with part of my Nobel Peace Prize money to be distributed now, to people representing different regions (all the continents of the world are represented here) during this Kalachakra gathering. These seeds have been kept near the Kalachakra mandala for purification and blessings. Since these include seeds of apricot, walnut, papaya, guava, etc., suitable for planting under varying geographical conditions, experts in respective places should be consulted on their planting and care and, thus, you all should see my sincere aspiration is fulfilled."

From a speech at the Kalachakra Initiation at Sarnath, India, on December 29, 1990, when His Holiness distributed seeds of fruit-bearing trees to encourage environmental protection through planting.

" In contemporary human society, we do not lack knowledge, but the persistence of problems that are our own creation clearly demonstrates that we lack effective solutions to these problems. The obstacle to solving these problems is the presence of the human mind of excessive self-centeredness, attachment, anger, greed, discrimination, envy, competitiveness, and so on. Such problems also stem from deficits in our consideration of others, compassion, tolerance, conscientiousness, insight, and so on."

" Although science has not concerned itself with the enhancement of ethics and the cultivation of basic human values such as kindness, since science has emerged as a means to serve humanity, it should never be completely divorced from the values that are of great importance to the flourishing of human society. In Indian philosophical traditions in general, and in Buddhism in particular, one finds many techniques for training the mind, such as the cultivation of calm abiding (*samatha*) and insight (*vipasyana*)."

From His Holiness' introduction to Science and Philosophy in the Indian Buddhist Classics, Vol. 2: The Mind. *The original Tibetan version by His Holiness was translated into English by Thupten Jinpa.*

Left:
His Holiness planting a tree at Rajgiri, Bihar, India.

" Ethics is the lifeblood of human existence. When a body loses its lifeblood, it turns into a corpse. In the same way, if we lose our sense of ethics, we will be like a tree with dead roots."

Right:
His Holiness admiring flowers at his residence, McLeod Ganj.

Opposite:
Mountain landscape, high-altitude, Sichuan.

" What we need today is an approach to ethics which makes no recourse to religion and can be equally acceptable to those with faith and those without: a secular ethics. This statement may seem strange coming from someone who from a very early age has lived as a monk in robes. Yet I see no contradiction here.
My faith enjoins me to strive for the welfare and benefit of all sentient beings, and reaching out beyond my own tradition, to those of other religions and those of none, is entirely in keeping with this …

I am confident that it is both possible and worthwhile to attempt a new secular approach to universal ethics. My confidence comes from my conviction that all of us, all human beings, are basically inclined or disposed toward what we perceive to be good. Whatever we do, we do because we think it will be of some benefit. At the same time, we all appreciate the kindness of others. We are all, by nature, oriented toward the basic human values of love and compassion. We all prefer the love of others to their hatred. We all prefer others' generosity to their meanness. And who among us does not prefer tolerance, respect, and forgiveness of our failings to bigotry, disrespect, and resentment?"

— *Beyond Religion: Ethics for a Whole World*

" When I am at home, I enjoy morning walks and looking at the beautiful flowers in my garden. The row of stout cherry trees at my residence produces exquisite blossoms every year. They are the result of the tiny saplings that I brought back from Japan fifty years ago — so they have seen most of my life in exile."

> "Science, for all the benefits it has brought to our external world, has not yet provided scientific grounding for the development of the foundations of personal integrity — the basic inner human values that we appreciate in others and would do well to promote in ourselves ..."
>
> — *Beyond Religion: Ethics for a Whole World*

> [If Buddha returned to this world] Buddha would be green …
> [If I joined a political party now] I would like to join the Green Party. I think their idea is good.

> Our life will become meaningless the day we lose the value of justice and ethics. We all have an equal right to pursue happiness. No one wants pain and suffering. Justice and equality are the unique prerogatives of human beings. We should not sacrifice these principles in the pursuit of power or material wealth. Instead, we should use these prerogatives to serve others' interests. But to do so, we need a firm foundation of ethics. If we are not guided by a sense of ethics and morality, our action tends to seek our self-interest, to the detriment of others.

Opposite:
Tibetan monks, Ganze, Sichuan.

Above:
Leafy Buddha painting by Tashi Norbu.

— *Gems from the Heart,* Tibetan Women's Association, 2005

Sacred Landscape

"For over 1,000 years we Tibetans have adhered to spiritual and environmental values in order to maintain the delicate balance of life across the high plateau on which we live. Inspired by the Buddha's message of non-violence and compassion and protected by our mountains, we have sought to respect every form of life, while our neighbors lived undisturbed."

An Essay on Mountains, *Newsweek, July 16, 1992*

> When we look back at our own country, Tibet, it is a big country with a vast land area, with high altitude and a cold and dry climate. Perhaps these things provided some kind of natural protection to Tibet's environment — keeping it clean and fresh. In the Northern pastures, the rocky areas, the forested areas and the river valleys there used to be lots of wild animals, fish and birds. As a Buddhist country there were certain traditional laws in Tibet concerned with a complete ban on fishing and hunting.

Previous Page:
Prayer flags at the sacred peak of Kawakarpo, Yunnan.

Opposite:
Yaks grazing at high summer nomad camp, Tibet.

Left:
Lake Namtso, a vast sacred lake in central Tibet, requires a lengthy period of time for a complete walking circuit.

"Even in Lhasa, one did not feel in any way cut off from the natural world. In my rooms at the top of the Potala, the winter palace of the Dalai Lamas, I spent countless hours as a child studying the behaviour of the red-beaked *khyungkar* which nested in the crevices of its walls. And behind the Norbulingka, the summer palace, I often saw pairs of *trung trung* (black-necked cranes), birds which for me are the epitome of elegance and grace, that lived in the marshlands there."

"In some of our songs, we symbolise them [black-necked cranes] as sacred ... In the old days, I used to see many pairs of cranes nesting in Lhasa in the marshes behind the Norbulingka. I have heard they are gone now."

Opposite:
Chortens near the Potala Palace, Lhasa, at dawn.

"In Tibet, mountains are often considered the abodes of deities. For example, Amnye Machen, a mountain in northeastern Tibet, is regarded as the home of Machen Pomra, one of the most important deities of Amdo, my home province. Because all the people of Amdo consider Machen Pomra their special friend, many of them go round the foot of the mountain on pilgrimage."

— *Newsweek, July 16, 1992*

"In Tibet, wildlife was protected in accordance with Buddhist principles. In the seventeenth century, we began enacting decrees to protect the environment and so we may have been one of the first nations to have difficulty enforcing environmental regulations!"

Opposite:
Landscape near Amnye Machen region.

Right:
Monks on pilgrimage to Lhamo Lhatso, east Tibet. This small lake is where divinations were conducted for clues to find the present 14th Dalai Lama.

"In Tibet, before the Chinese occupation, ... areas near lakes controlled by the Tibetan government had a rich bird life. The government assigned and paid people to safeguard these birds and their eggs. Environmental protection in those days was not spurred by the kind of preservation awareness we have today. It was rather influenced by the Buddha's teaching of safeguarding the life of all living beings."

"When the forests in Tibet die, the whole nation suffers. And when a people suffers, the whole world suffers. We need forests for our health as well. When we go for a walk in a forest, fresh air is healing. We need green forests. They are nature's great gift. Forests are good for our soul. In the forests we find the calm that our own brain needs for regeneration. Forests are water reservoirs, home to many animal and plant species, and are important as an air-conditioning machine. They are a mirror of the diversity of life. The large-scale deforestation in Tibet is a matter of great sadness."

Previous Page:
The majestic Lake Yamdrok Tso, in central Tibet, occupies a special place in Tibetan lore as it is connected with the origin of Tibet. Chinese engineers desecrated the lake by building a pumped-storage dam at the lake-side in the 1990s.

Left:
Wildflower meadows in east Tibet.

Opposite:
Tibetan monastery in Sichuan protects the forest in the vicinity.

"We always considered our wild animals a symbol of freedom. Nothing held them back, they ran free. Without them something is missing from even the most beautiful landscape. The land becomes empty, and only with the presence of wild animals can it gain its full beauty. Nature and wild animals are complementary. People who live among wildlife without harming it are in harmony with the environment. Sadly, the profusion of wildlife that once thrived in the region is no longer to be found."

Opposite:
Yaks grazing on high slopes of Kangshung Valley, Everest region, Tibet. Yaks forage on grasses, lichens, moss and herbs, keeping the grasslands in good shape.

Right:
The Tibetan Antelope (chiru) was hunted to near-extinction for its underwool (shahtoosh), the finest wool in the world. Numbers are slowly recovering after the trade in shahtoosh was internationally banned, but poaching still goes on.

"As a young man, I recall seeing great numbers of different species whenever I travelled outside Lhasa. My chief memory of the three-month journey across Tibet from my birthplace at Takster in the East to Lhasa, where I was formally proclaimed Dalai Lama as a four-year-old boy, is of the wildlife we encountered along the way. Immense herds of *kiang* (wild asses) and *drong* (wild yaks) freely roamed the great plains. Occasionally we would catch sight of shimmering herds of *gowa*, the shy Tibetan gazelle, *shawa-chakar*, the white-lipped deer, or of *tsoe*, our magnificent antelope. I remember, too, my fascination for the little *chibi*, or pika, which would congregate on grassy areas. They were so friendly. I loved to watch the birds: the dignified *gho* (the bearded eagle) soaring high above the monasteries and perched up in the mountains; the flocks of geese (*nangbar*); and occasionally at night, to hear the call of the *wookpa* (the long-eared owl)."

From HH Dalai Lama's journey to Lhasa, in July 1939. Quoted from his book Ancient Wisdom, Modern World, *(1999).*

Left:
Blue sheep on a high peak in Sikkim

Opposite:
The Tibetan Wild Ass (kyang) has never been tamed. Once found in vast herds on the grasslands of Tibet, this animal is now only found in smaller groups scattered across the plateau. Tibet's wildlife was slaughtered to the brink of extinction by Chinese settlers and military in the 1960s and 1970s.
Photo from Changtang region, northern Tibet

" In the old days, Tibet had an abundance of wildlife. Animals such as kiang (wild ass), tsoe (Tibetan antelope), gowa (Tibetan gazelle), naa (blue sheep), drong (wild yak) could be found in large numbers. Over the decades, however, many of these animals have been hunted. As a result, some of them have now become extinct."

> Only hermits, wild animals, and, in the summer, nomads and their herds actually live high amongst them, but in the simplicity and quiet of our mountains, there is more peace of mind than in most cities of the world. Since the practice of Buddhism involves seeing phenomena as empty of inherent existence, it is helpful for a meditator to be able to look into the vast, empty space seen from a mountain-top.

Opposite:
A Tibetan nomad on pilgrimage fills up on water from sacred Lake Manasarovar — not for drinking, but to take home for the home altar.

Above:
Lake Manasarovar, Tibet.

> Many Indians I think maybe more than thousand years — they are very eager having the pilgrimage to that area [Mount Kailash and Lake Manasarovar]. So I usually teasing those Indian pilgrims, what is their experience? Because of high altitude and very cold, so naturally, they find very very difficult. So then their usual answer: [on a] spiritual level, very happy — they also have some extraordinary sort of experience. But on a physical level, very cold. And on top of that, according to their tradition, they have to swim, they have to take bath in the Manasarovar water. Very cold! Almost frozen. That's [the] obvious sort of blessing of the pilgrimage of that area.

Above:
Tibetan pilgrims on kora (walking circuit) of Mount Kailash. The circuit can be completed in one lengthy day by hardy Tibetans. Westerners are more likely to take three or four days for the arduous loop.

"Ancient cultures that have adapted to their natural surroundings can offer special insights on structuring human societies to exist in balance with the environment. For example, Tibetans are uniquely familiar with life on the Himalayan plateau. This has evolved into a long history of a civilization that took care not to overwhelm and destroy its fragile eco-system. Tibetans have long appreciated the presence of wild animals as symbolic of freedom."

"I just wish to emphasize the obvious and undisputed fact that we Tibetans are a distinct people with our own culture, language, religion and history. But for China's occupation, Tibet would still, today, fulfill its natural role as a buffer state maintaining and promoting peace in Asia."

Left:
Tibetan nomad moving camp.

Above:
Tibetan nomads and their yaks moving over snow in winter.

Center:
Nomad woman with rosy cheeks — which come from windburn.

Opposite:
Inside a nomad yak-hair tent, with yak-dung providing fuel for the stove.

"During the 11th century, the famous Tibetan practitioner the great yogi Milarepa spent many years at Mount Kailash. Many great practitioners when they spend time at that sacred mountain, certain unusual visions happen... [In] my own case, I have never been there, so when people tell me about their experiences, sometimes, you see, a little bit jealous!"

> Travelers in Tibet traditionally add a stone to the cairns at the tops of hills or passes with a shout of "*Lha-gyal-lo*" (Victory to the gods). Later, 'Mani stones', stones carved with prayers and other scriptures may be added along with prayer flags. One practical outcome of this traditional sense for the environment is a deep-seated concern to protect it.

An Essay on Mountains, *Newsweek*, July 16, 1992

Previous Page:
Chiu Gompa is one of the temples located along the walking circuit around Mount Kailash, the peak appearing here. The 6714-metre peak has never been summited, out of respect for the powerful deities said to reside there.

Opposite:
Prayer-flags fluttering in east Nepal, with peaks of Kangtega and Thamserku towering behind.

Top:
Mantras carved on mani stones, Ladakh.

Above:
Painting a fresco of a deity on a rock near sacred site.

"The Tibetan plateau would be transformed into the world's largest natural park or biosphere. Strict laws would be enforced to protect wildlife and plant life; the exploitation of natural resources would be carefully regulated so as not to damage relevant ecosystems; and a policy of sustainable development would be adopted in populated areas....

Tibet's height and size (the size of the European Community), as well as its unique history and profound spiritual heritage makes it ideally suited to fulfill the role of a sanctuary of peace in the strategic heart of Asia."

HH Dalai Lama's vision for Tibet, from his Nobel Acceptance Speech, December 1989

Opposite:
Prayer-flags fluttering in Everest region: photo taken from Gokyo Ri, Nepal.

Next Page
Lake Yamdrok Tso, central Tibet, with snowcaps visible on the Tibet-Bhutan border.

"In the remoteness of the Himalayas
In the days of yore, the land of Tibet
Observed a ban on hunting, on fishing
And, during designated periods, even construction
These traditions are noble
For they preserve and cherish
The lives of humble, helpless, defenseless creatures."

Stanza from The Sheltering Tree of Interdependence

Preserving the Third Pole

" This blue planet is our only home and Tibet is its roof. As vital as the Arctic and Antarctic, it is the Third Pole. The Tibetan Plateau needs to be protected, not just for Tibetans but for the environmental health and sustainability of the entire world. "

"Sooner or later, China will need to follow the worldwide trend toward democracy and freedom. In the long run, China cannot escape truth, justice and freedom either. My hope and vision is for Tibet to become a demilitarized zone of peace and non-violence between the two major powers of China and India. My homeland now has major environmental problems. The reason the ecological problems are so serious is because Tibet is the upland that is the source of all the great rivers of Asia such as the Brahmaputra, the Yellow River, the Ganges, and the Mekong. And if this area is contaminated, that has negative consequences for two billion people. We know that nuclear waste is stored in some regions of Tibet. Certainly there are also atom bombs stationed in parts of Tibet. Needless to say, nuclear power plants have a negative impact on the environment. Tibet's forests are also being clear-cut, causing widespread deforestation. Meanwhile, mineral resources are being rapidly exploited and depleted."

Previous Page:
Sunrise, Kangshung Face of Everest, Tibet.

Above:
Everest, Lhotse & Western Cwm shot through an optical window on the photographer's own light aircraft.

Right:
From summit of Everest, looking into Tibet toward Rongbuk Glacier. This was Mountaineer Pat Morrow's first glimpse of Tibet — having summited Everest from the Nepalese side.

"In this respect, I always say, Tibet is usually called the Roof of the World. According to some experts, because of Tibet's high altitude and dry climate, if its ecology is damaged, it takes a much longer time to recover. So therefore, environment situation in such an area is very delicate."

Opposite:
Glaciers and snowpack at Kharta glacier, Everest region.

Right:
Mt Everest reflected in a melted glacial pool, near Rongbuk, Tibet.

"Look at those big ices in North and South Pole, the amount of melting is also very serious. And snow mountains and glaciers in Tibet are also rapidly melting. Basically, I am not an expert but I have serious concern about that."

"I believe that the achievement of Tenzing Sherpa, who accompanied Edmund Hillary on the first ascent of Everest, the world's highest mountain, in 1953, is a similarly inspiring story. For conquering a mountain peak requires not only great physical stamina, but also the possession of great courage, loyalty and trust, a concern for your companions greater than the natural urge for self-preservation. These are qualities that I believe he possessed in abundance. Even today, many years after the event, adults and children alike marvel that Tenzing and Hillary were able to reach the highest point on earth. It has become a standard of human success."

From HH Dalai Lama's Foreword to Tenzing and the Sherpas of Everest, *by Tashi Tenzing and Judy Tenzing. Photo shows mountaineers' advanced camp at Everest, Nepal side.*

"You know, in Tibet we have big mountains. I think, if Tibet be free, we have good skiing!"

His Holiness excited about witnessing the sport of skiing, during a visit to Santa Fe, New Mexico, in 1991.

Top:
Mountaineers' advanced camp at Everest, Nepal side.

Above:
An expedition mountaineer on Nordic skis at Rongbuk Glacier, Tibetan side of Everest.

"In my lifetime glaciers have melted and snow on the mountains has reduced. Natural disasters associated with global warming have increased. I don't know to what extent human lifestyle has affected this, but we have to look into what effective actions we can take."

" I heard that due to forced settlement of Nomads nowadays into permanent houses built specially for them have lots of negative impacts on the environment. Many of Tibetan traditions, especially those of nomadic traditions from thousands of years are naturally very sustainable with environment. For example, Yak dung is used as fuel in cooking fire and it is also helpful for the enriching the nutrients of soils. Yaks hoof are useful for grasses as well."

" Life is as dear to a mute creature as it is to a man. Just as one wants happiness and fears pain, just as one wants to live and not to die, so do other creatures."

" Killing animals for sport, for pleasure, for adventure, and for hides and furs is a phenomenon which is at once disgusting and distressing. There is no justification in indulging in such acts of brutality."

Opposite:
The vast grasslands of Tibet act as a carbon sink, keeping moisture in the soil, and holding a lid on methane trapped below in permafrost. This is not a natural system: the grasslands of Tibet have evolved over millennia with yaks and grazing wildlife.

Above:
Nomad woman milking a Nak.

Right:
Snow leopard pelts on sale in Kashgar, Xinjiang. Snow leopard parts are used for Traditional Chinese Medicinal bogus cures, the same as tigers.

"Tibetans have a great respect for all forms of life. This inherent feeling is enhanced by the Buddhist faith, which prohibits the harming of all sentient beings, whether human or animal. Prior to the Chinese invasion, Tibet was an unspoiled wilderness sanctuary in a unique natural environment. Sadly, in the past decades the wildlife and the forests of Tibet have been almost totally destroyed by the Chinese. The effects on Tibet's delicate environment have been devastating. What little is left in Tibet must be protected and efforts must be made to restore the environment to its balanced state."

Left:
Nomad family on the move.

Opposite:
Mixed farming and grazing in a valley in eastern Tibet.

> One aspect is ecology. Lots of damage is done inside Tibet. Firstly, lot of deforestation and then secondly, exploiting natural resources extremely without caring about the impact on environment. Some of my Indian friends say that, because of high altitude and dry climate, once the ecology is damaged, it takes longer period to recover. So the Tibetan ecology is quite delicate.

Above:
Bulldozing Tibet: extensive Chinese mining operations across Tibet are severely damaging the grassland ecosystem.

Right:
A makeshift concrete settlement for Tibetan nomads who have been forced to give up their nomadic ways and either sell their yaks or send them to the slaughterhouse. Over 2 million Tibetan nomads have been forcibly settled since 1990.

“ According to Chinese statistics there are 126 different minerals in Tibet. When these resources were discovered by the Chinese, they were extensively mined without proper environmental safeguards, resulting in devastation of the environment. As a result, deforestation and mining are causing more floods in the lowlands of Tibet. ”

Left:
A Tibetan yak-hair tent faces off with Chinese mountain-top mining. Mountain tops are considered the abodes of deities by Tibetans — places to be left untouched.

Above:
Asbestos mining by Chinese operator, NE Tibet

"Because of the growth in the population, a large number of trees are cut for fuel, and to reclaim land for agricultural cultivation. In the case of Tibet, too, the Chinese have now destroyed its ancient trees in a similar way to shaving a man's head off. This is not simply the destruction of trees but it also means harming what belongs to the Tibetans."

"We needlessly pollute
The fair bosom of our mother earth
Rip out her trees to feed our short-sighted greed
Turning our fertile earth into a sterile desert"

Left:
Slopes of Kham, east Tibet, where old-growth forest has been extensively logged by Chinese companies, often illegally.

Above:
Chinese logging truck, Kham, east Tibet

Opposite:
Winter at Tibetan monastic encampment of Yarchen Gar, Sichuan, in better days. A large section of this Buddhist study enclave was demolished by Chinese officials, suspicious of large gatherings.

Next Page:
Winter snow coats Kongur Sand Dunes, Sevrei Mountains, Gobi Desert, (outer) Mongolia. Creeping desertification is a huge problem across China, Mongolia and Tibet.
Photo by Colin Monteath

"Scientists say that due to global warming, many parts of the world could become desert. That is very serious. Dr Yuan T. Lee, a Taiwanese Nobel laureate in Chemistry, told me that after another eighty years the world will be like a desert. He said that water resources are diminishing alarmingly. Therefore, we all need to modify our lifestyle, abandoning fossil fuels and turning to renewable sources of energy."

Asia's Lifeline

" Ten major rivers which cover almost whole Asia, their ultimate source come from Tibetan plateau. Therefore, I think over a billion Human Beings life depends on these rivers, so it is very important. "

"In these stores of natural treasure our doctors found many of the precious herbs and plants from which they compounded their medicines, while nomads found rich pasture for their animals, so crucial to the Tibetan economy. But of even wider-ranging impact, the Land of Snow's mountains are the source of many of Asia's great rivers."

Previous Page:
The Mekong River in Laos. There are a dozen Chinese megadams upstream, severely disrupting not only the flow of the river but the passage of nutrient-rich silt as well as disrupting fish migration and spawning.

Right:
The Mekong close to its source in Tibet runs a glacial blue. As it picks up huge amounts of sediment, the river turns murky brown. The nutrient-rich sediment is increasingly trapped by China's cascade of megadams on the Mekong in Yunnan — which represents a food security nightmare for the nations downstream.

Opposite:
The Kali Gandaki river snakes down from the Tibetan border to Kagbeni in Nepal, where crops depend on the waters.

Opposite:
A Western explorer rappels down a rock-face to get closer to thundering Hidden Falls. First surveyed in 1998, Hidden Falls is estimated to be around 33 metres (or 108 feet) tall—the highest yet discovered on the mighty Yarlung Tsangpo.

Above:
In eastern Tibet, the Yarlung Tsangpo River suddenly changes direction. This region is known as the Great Bend. Due to tremendous drop in elevation, the river here holds highest hydropower potential on the planet.

Chinese engineers plan to construct a cascade of dams here to tap into 70 GW of output, likely destroying the river in the process.

"Within this century, I think tremendous sort of difficulties — like drinking water ... These are unthinkable negative consequences. Although these big rivers [from Tibet] create some problems due to flood, if the waters dry, that will be more disaster. So I think we need special care about Tibetan environment. So our friends [from] outside world — American, European, Asian, particularly Indian — please help us materialise a meaningful solution or dialogue with the Chinese government. In order to achieve that, it is important to educate our Chinese brothers and sisters what's the reality."

"[In Tibet] A small population inhabited a very large area with clean, dry air and an abundance of pure mountain water. This innocent attitude toward cleanliness meant that when we Tibetans went into exile, we were astonished to discover, for example, the existence of streams whose water is not drinkable."

Right:
Tibet is home to the highest peaks on the planet — and also the deepest gorges on earth. This is a gorge along the Salween, one of the last freeflowing rivers sourced in Tibet.

Opposite:
A kayaker tackles powerful whitewater on the Parlung Tsangpo, a tributary of the mighty Yarlung Tsangpo.

" ... many of the rivers which flow through large areas of Asia, through Pakistan, India, China, Vietnam, Laos and Cambodia, rivers such as the Yellow River, Brahmaputra, Yangtse, Salween and Mekong, all originate in Tibet.

It is at the places of origin of these rivers that large-scale deforestation and mining are taking place. The pollution of these rivers has a drastic effect on the downstream countries."

" Tibet has been regarded as the 'Water Tower of Asia' with majority of the major rivers originating from Tibetan glacial reserves, most of which are now at risk due to global warming as well as rampant damming of rivers by China affecting downstream countries adversely."

Above Left: Xiaowan Dam is part of an 11-megadam cascade that is effectively strangling the Mekong River in Yunnan, SW China. In terms of height and width, Xiaowan is over twice the size of the Potala Palace. The megadam is 292 metres tall, with capacity output of 4,200 MW. Its reservoir stretches back over 160 km and impounds a maximum of 14.6 billion cubic metres of water.

Above Right: Megadam under construction on the upper Yangtse River. Sourced in Tibet, the Yangtse is the most heavily dammed river in the world, and home to the world's largest dam, the colossal Three Gorges Dam. The Three Gorges Corporation continues to build colossal dams along the Yangtse and its tributaries.

"This is because Asia's major rivers rise in Tibet and more than 1 billion people depend on their waters. Damming the Brahmaputra, for example, will have effects on both India and Bangladesh."

Opposite:
Winnowing grain, Photoskar, Ladakh

Right:
Harvesting wheat near the banks of the Brahmaputra, Assam, India

"When we talk about water and the river, of course, spiritually, something very sacred [River Ganges], anyways, several crores [10 Millions] of people's lives depend upon these waters or rivers. So we must take special care about these rivers."

Left:
First ritual bath in the sacred River Ganges Varanasi, India.

Above:
Water-intensive rice farming, Bangladesh.

Opposite:
Accessing clean water often requires considerable time and effort, Bangladesh.

> "The dangers of fire, water and wind are limitless
> Sweltering heat dries up our lush forests
> Lashing our world with unprecedented storms
> And the oceans surrender their salt to the elements."

Stanza from The Sheltering Tree of Interdependence

Above:
Drought conditions in Mekong Delta, Vietnam.

Right:
This is a global issue.

Opposite:
The Mekong river near its source in Amdo, Tibet.

Next Page:
Fishing at Khone Phapheng Falls, Laos.

LIVE INTERVIEW

While printed versions translated from HH Dalai Lama's Tibetan original come out in flawless English, a live interview is a very different story. Live interviews reveal a very different cadence: the Laughing Bodhisattva. His Holiness could well be giggling his way through serious subjects — or bursting into gales of laughter.

The video links here derive from a documentary released in late 2020 by Hawaiian filmmaker Tom Vendetti, titled: *Dalai Lama China Mount Kailash Happiness*. The interviews date to circa 2015.

HH Dalai Lama talks about rivers sourced in Tibet
vimeo.com/548692741

HH Dalai Lama on pilgrimage to Kailash & Manasarovar
vimeo.com/548690348

MAJOR RIVERS SOURCED IN TIBET

www.MeltdowninTibet.com © Michael Buckley

Thinking Globally

" … let's remember that we depend on each other and that to meet the challenge of climate change, we have to work together. "

"One of the most powerful visions I have experienced was the first photograph of the Earth from outer space. The image of a blue planet floating in deep space, glowing like the full moon on a clear night, brought home powerfully to me the recognition that we are indeed all members of a single family sharing one little house.

The earth is, to a certain extent, our mother. She is so kind, because whatever we do, she tolerates it. But now, the time has come when our power to destroy is so extreme that Mother Earth is compelled to tell us to be careful. The population explosion and many other indications make that clear, don't they? Nature has its own natural limitations.

Today, all over the world, including Tibet, ecological degradation is fast overtaking us. I am wholly convinced that, if all of us do not make a concerted effort, with a sense of universal responsibility, we will see the gradual breakdown of the fragile ecosystems that support us, resulting in an irreversible and irrevocable degradation of our planet, Earth.

Climate change is not the concern of just one or two nations. It is an issue that affects the whole of humanity and every living being on this earth. This beautiful planet is our only home. If, due to global warming and other environmental problems, the earth cannot sustain itself, there is no other planet to which we can move. We have to take serious action now to protect our environment and find constructive solutions to global warming.

When we see photographs of the Earth from space, we see no boundaries between us, just this one blue planet. This is no longer a time to think only of 'my nation' or 'our continent' alone. There is a real need for a greater sense of global responsibility based on a sense of the oneness of humanity."

Message to delegates of COP24 UN Climate Conference, *November 20, 2018.*

Above:
NASA image

> The world belongs to its 7 billion inhabitants. In the past, communities could flourish in isolation, but now we can't. This World Environment Day, let's remember that we depend on each other and that to meet the challenge of climate change, we have to work together.

World Environment Day, June 5, 2018

> Our ancestors viewed the earth as rich and bountiful, which it is. Many people in the past also saw nature as inexhaustibly sustainable, which we now know is the case only if we care for it.

Left:

Located on the Yellow River, the Inner Mongolia city of Wuhai used to be based around grapes, wine-making, and dairy farming. Now, because Inner Mongolia holds over 25% of China's coal reserves, its economy is based around coal mining, power plants, and chemical industries. There is intense pollution.

Above:

Snowcapped peak in east Tibet

"... what is clear is that we are the only species with the power to destroy the earth. Birds and insects have no such power, nor does any other mammal. And yet if we have the capacity to destroy the earth, we also have the capacity to protect it. I believe we have an urgent responsibility to do so."

"The big nations should pay more attention to ecology. I hope you see those big nations who spent a lot of money for weapons or war turn their resources to the preservation of the climate."

"We human beings, what is wrong with us? We human beings have such intelligence and human wisdom. I think we often use human intelligence in a wrong way or direction. As a result, in a way, we are doing certain actions which essentially go against basic human nature."

EARTH DAY, 22 April 2020.
A message from HH Dalai Lama during Coronavirus crisis

"On this 50th anniversary of Earth Day, our planet is facing one of the greatest challenges to the health and well-being of its people. And yet, in the midst of this struggle, we are reminded of the value of compassion and mutual support. The current global pandemic threatens us all, without distinctions of race, culture or gender, and our response must be as one humanity, providing for the most essential needs of all.

Whether we like it or not, we have been born on this earth as part of one great family. Rich or poor, educated or uneducated, belonging to one nation or another, ultimately each of us is just a human being like everyone else. Furthermore, we all have the same right to pursue happiness and avoid suffering. When we recognize that all beings are equal in this respect, we automatically feel empathy and closeness towards others. Out of this comes a genuine sense of universal responsibility: the wish to actively help others overcome their problems.

Our Mother Earth is teaching us a lesson in universal responsibility. This blue planet is a delightful habitat. Its life is our life; its future, our future. Indeed, the earth acts like a mother to us all; as her children, we are dependent on her. In the face of the global problems we are going through it is important that we must all work together. I came to appreciate the importance of environmental concern only after escaping from Tibet in 1959, where we always considered the environment to be pure. Whenever we saw a stream of water, for instance, there was no worry about whether it was safe to drink. Sadly, the mere availability of clean drinking water is a major problem throughout the world today.

We must ensure that the sick and the valiant health-care providers throughout the world have access to the fundamental necessities of clean water and proper sanitation to prevent the uncontrolled spread of disease. Hygiene is one of the bases of effective health care. Sustainable access to properly equipped and staffed health-care facilities will help us meet the challenges of the current pandemic that ravages our planet. It will also offer one of the strongest defenses against future public health crises. I understand that these are precisely the objectives set forth in the United Nations Sustainable Development Goals that address challenges to global health.

As we face this crisis together, it is imperative that we act in a spirit of solidarity and cooperation in order to provide for the pressing needs, particularly of our less fortunate brothers and sisters around the world. I hope and pray that in the days ahead, each of us will do all we can to create a happier and healthier world."

"In this time of great fear, it is important that we think of the long-term challenges — and possibilities — of the entire globe. Photographs of the world from space clearly show that there are no real boundaries on our blue planet. Therefore, all of us must take care of it and work to prevent climate change and other destructive forces. This pandemic serves as a warning that only by coming together with a coordinated global response will we meet the unprecedented challenges we face."

At the time of the Coronavirus pandemic,
TIME Magazine,
April 14, 2020

"East, west, north, south: everyone is interdependent. The modern economy has no national boundaries. Therefore, now we need a sense of oneness of all 7 billion human beings. In the past, many problems were created because of too much emphasis on our differences, such as nationalities and religions. Now, in modern times, that thinking is out of date. We should think about humanity, about the whole world.

We must listen to scientists and specialists. Their voices and knowledge are very important. And religious people should pay more attention to scientists rather than just pray, pray, pray. In the ancient Nalanda Buddhist tradition, which we Tibetans follow, everything is investigated and not accepted by faith alone. If through reasoning we find some contradiction, even in Buddha's own words, then we have the right to reject them. From childhood, I was always engaged in a lot of debate. Our thinking was based not in faith but reasoning."

"Human beings
And countless beings
That inhabit water and land
Reel under the yoke of physical pain
Caused by malevolent diseases
Their minds are dulled
With sloth, stupor and ignorance
The joys of the body and spirit
Are far, far away."

Stanza from The Sheltering Tree of Interdependence

Opposite:
HH Dalai Lama at Bodhgaya, India

"This planet is our only home. Environmental experts say that over the next few decades, global warming will reach such a level that many water resources will go dry. So ecology and combatting global warming are very important."

EARTH DAY, 22 April 2021.
A message from HH Dalai Lama

"On Earth Day 2021, I appeal to my brothers and sisters throughout the world to look at both the challenges and the opportunities before us on this one blue planet that we share.

I often joke that the moon and stars look beautiful, but if any of us tried to live on them, we would be miserable. This planet of ours is a delightful habitat. Its life is our life, its future our future. Indeed, the earth acts like a mother to us all. Like children, we are dependent on her. In the face of such global problems as the effect of global heating and depletion of the ozone layer, individual organizations and single nations are helpless. Unless we all work together, no solution can be found. Our mother earth is teaching us a lesson in universal responsibility.

Take the issue of water as an example. Today, more than ever, the welfare of citizens in many parts of the world, especially of mothers and children, is at extreme risk because of the critical lack of adequate water, sanitation and hygienic conditions. It is concerning that the absence of these essential health services throughout the world impacts nearly two billion people. And yet it is soluble. I am grateful that the Secretary-General of the United Nations, Antonio Guterres, has issued an urgent global call to action.

Interdependence is a fundamental law of nature. Ignorance of interdependence has wounded not just our natural environment, but our human society as well. Therefore, we human beings must develop a greater sense of the oneness of all humanity. Each of us must learn to work not only for his or her self, family or nation, but for the benefit of all mankind. In this connection, I am glad that President Joe Biden will be hosting a Leaders' Climate Summit on Earth Day this year, bringing together world leaders to discuss an issue that impacts all of us.

If our planet is to be sustained, environmental education and personal responsibility must grow and keep growing. Taking care of the environment should be an essential part of our daily lives. In my own case, my environmental awakening occurred only after I came into exile and encountered a world very different from the one I had known in Tibet. Only then did I realize how pure the Tibetan environment was and how modern material development has contributed to the degradation of life across the planet.

On this Earth Day let us all commit ourselves to doing our part to help make a positive difference to the environment of our only common home, this beautiful Earth."

Opposite:
Mt Kanchenjunga, which at 8586m is the world's third highest peak, and the jewel of Kanchenjunga National Park, a World Heritage Site. Photo taken from Gangtok, Sikkim. Sikkim has devoted a large part of its land area to national parks and nature reserves.

Call to Action

" Change only takes place through action. Frankly speaking, not through prayer or meditation, but through action. "

" An international movement for climate justice has arisen across the world, from North America to the Philippines, from New Zealand to India to Norway, demanding that governments and big businesses take responsibility for their impact on the environment. You, today's young citizens, are pioneering climate justice, aware of the fact that you are directly concerned and it is your future that is at stake. The fact that so many of you are engaged with these issues gives me confidence in my optimism for the future.

The problems facing you, whether to do with climate change, violence in general and terrorism in particular, were not created by God, Buddha or extraterrestrials. They did not fall from the sky, or rise up from the ground. Humanity is entirely responsible for being at the root of the problems that have caused these crises. Which is good news. Because if we have created these problems, it is logical to believe that we have the means to resolve them. The crises facing us today are not inevitable. Ask yourselves: 'What if fraternity were to be our response to these crises?' "

" Over the years, since our first arriving in exile, I have taken a close interest in environmental issues. The Tibetan government in exile has paid particular attention to introducing our children to their responsibilities as residents of this fragile planet. And I never hesitate to speak out on the subject whenever I am given the opportunity. In particular, I always stress the need to consider how our actions, in affecting the environment, are likely to affect others. I admit that this is very often difficult to judge. "

— *Ancient Wisdom, Modern World*

Previous Page:
Protesters in New Delhi, India, 2019, taking part in global climate strike.

> And above all, be the generation that acts. You may be the first generation in history to face the very real possibility of the extinction of life on our shared planet, but you are also the last one that will be able to do something about it.

> Environmental education about the consequences of the destruction of our ecosystem and the dramatic decrease in biodiversity must be given top priority. But creating awareness is not sufficient; we must find ways to bring about changes in the way we live. I call on the younger generation — be rebels demanding climate protection and climate justice because it is your future that is at stake. One of the most positive recent developments has been the growing awareness that we have to act. Seventeen-year-old Greta Thunberg, the teenage environmental activist who insists we heed scientists' warnings and take direct action, inspires me. Millions of young people have been moved by her example to protest governments' inaction over the climate crisis.

> People have elected greater numbers of Green parliamentarians in Germany, Switzerland, Finland, Belgium, the Netherlands and the European Parliament. This is a good indication that public opinion and actions can change politicians' minds. I often have the impression that politicians do not take climate and environmental protection seriously enough. Ignorance is the Number One enemy. It is not sufficient to hold meetings and conferences. We must set a timetable for change. Only if political leaders start to act now will we have reason to hope. We must not sacrifice our civilization for the greed of the few.

Opposite:
Tibetan protesters take part in global climate strike in McLeod Ganj, India, 2019.

Taking care of our planet is a matter of looking after our own home. We can no longer exploit the earth's resources — the trees, water, air and minerals — with no care for coming generations. I support young people's protests at governments' inaction over the climate crisis.

" Human beings are responsible for much of climate change; we therefore have the responsibility to take care before it becomes irreversible. I have made environmental conservation one of my life's commitments: I advocate protection of the environment wherever I go. The older people will probably be able to manage over the next several decades; however, we must think about how life will be for our future generation.

It is encouraging that members of today's younger generation, such as Greta Thunberg, have serious concerns about the climate crisis and its effects on the environment. Mother Earth is our only home. It is therefore important that we all take better care of it before it is too late. "

Message to the Swedish-Tibetan School Culture Society for staging a Climate Gala event in Stockholm with the theme "Tibet is Melting", November 5, 2019.

Opposite:
The fallout from China's reckless policies in Tibet will result in 'climate refugees'—millions of them, in Tibet, in China and in the nations downstream. These protesters are taking part in a climate strike in New Delhi.

Far Left:
Tibet action group at COP25 climate conference in Madrid, December 2019, drove a van around with a quote from HH Dalai Lama featured on the side.

Left:
Protest in Delhi, India

" It is encouraging to see how you have opened the eyes of the world to the urgency to protect our planet, our only home. At the same time, you have inspired so many young brothers and sisters to join this movement."

HH Dalai Lama, writing to Greta Thunberg, May 31, 2019.

" We should pay more attention about ecology and preserve water resources… We really need a concept of oneness of 7 billion human beings. We all live on one planet. Our basic way of life is the same. So according to that reality, no longer emphasis on my nation, my country. Now we should think more of humanity."
"I think education is a key thing. Usually our thinking is short-sighted and narrow-minded: interest for myself and my community, my nation. The best way for your interest is to think about the well-being of humanity on this planet."

His Holiness speaking at Our Planet, Our Future, a virtual gathering of Nobel laureates, scientists, policy-makers and youth leaders, April 27, 2021. His Holiness signed a letter with 100 of his fellow Nobel laureates urging the phasing out of fossil fuels.

" So when I heard this young girl from Sweden. I really felt, "Oh, there's real hope from our younger generation, who's really thinking this environment and these things." So this is, I can attest, such a time. We generally will materialistic thinking and then finally, small circle, my nation, my community, as I briefly mentioned, so now it is quite rare who talking about world. About environment. These things. I really feel this a sign of hope for future. Like my generation now, ending. Like you, the younger generation really now all our hope depend on these young people."

From Live online discussion, January 9, 2021: HH Dalai Lama with Greta Thunberg and Leading Scientists: A Conversation on the Crisis of Climate Feedback Loops. This event marked the launch of 5 short films created by the Mind & Life Institute, co-founded by HH Dalai Lama.

" These days when we talk about preservation of the environment, whether we mean the wildlife, forests, oceans, rivers or mountains, ultimately the decision to act must come from our hearts. So, the key point, I think, is for all of us to develop a genuine sense of universal responsibility, not only towards this beautiful blue planet that is our home, but also towards the innumerable sentient beings with whom we share it."

An Essay on Mountains, *Newsweek, July 16, 1992.*

" The time for social, emotional and ethical learning has come. In today's world, we are all interconnected. The challenges that face us, and that will face future generations, require cooperation across national, ethnic, and religious boundaries. We must see each other not as adversaries or competitors for limited resources, but as brothers and sisters living together on the only planet we call home. Therefore, we need a new, up-to-date way of thinking, one that acknowledges our interdependence and the necessity of resolving problems and instigating changes through dialogue and collaboration. Our compassion cannot be limited only to those who look like us or who share our citizenship or religion; it must be extended to encompass everyone on the basis of our common humanity. All religions advocate compassion, but to involve the whole of humanity we need an ethical approach with universal appeal: a secular ethics that nurtures such basic human values as empathy, tolerance, forgiveness and love."

From HH Dalai Lama's foreword to the SEE Learning Companion, *January 23, 2019.*

In 2019, HH Dalai Lama launched the SEE Learning Curriculum in coordination with Emory University. SEE stands for Social, Emotional and Ethical Learning, with the initial audience being elementary and middle school students. The curriculum derives inspiration from HH Dalai Lama's books such as *Beyond Religion: Ethics for a Whole World*. The curriculum has been translated into a dozen languages.

"The establishment of a worldwide initiative to educate the heart and mind has been a long-cherished dream," he wrote.

Indeed, our survival on this planet may well depend on promoting the values that HH Dalai Lama holds dear — secular ethics, compassion, world peace, warm heartedness, universal responsibility, and working together globally. What is desperately needed is a shift of consciousness to tackle climate change.

"Hours, minutes and seconds: time never stands still. We also are part of that nature. The past is important, but already past. The future is still in our hands, so we must think about ecology at the global level."

Parting Shots
Environmental solutions from the Tibetan World

This section by
Michael Buckley, project editor

Tashi Norbu
བཀྲ་ཤིས་ནོར་བུ་

Above:
Ice stupa, Ladakh, Himalayan India — an ingenious artificial glacier, shown here in Phyang, built up from branches and pipes with the help of the local monastery and monks, and local people. An ice stupa stores winter water and releases it in spring, when water is very scarce but most needed. In this way, the Ice Stupa replicates the actions of a real glacier.
An ice stupa like this is consecrated by a Tibetan Rinpoche. Without the religious leaders on board, this ice stupa would not get built as it relies on local labour provided by villagers and monks. This pyramid of ice is the inspired vision of mechanical engineer Sonam Wangchuk, who runs ice stupa building competitions on a regular basis. A group of these ice stupas is enough to irrigate a whole valley during the summer. A full-sized stupa is ideally up to 40 metres high and can store up to 16,000 cubic metres of water—enough to irrigate ten hectares of land.

Left:
Buddha of the Third Pole —
Painting by Tashi Norbu

Left:

Solar power. Next to the Sahara, the Tibetan Plateau holds the highest potential for solar power on the planet, due to its high altitude. Above 4000 metres is above the treeline, so no wood is available at places like the isolated village in Zanskar. Previously, wood from Kashmir, and oil, diesel and gas from India would be hauled overland at great expense. Things have changed quite rapidly. All the hotels and households in Ladakh are using solar energy for lighting and water-heating while many of them are using solar cookers as well. Small solar power plants have been set up for remote villagers, monasteries, educational institutions and hospitals.

Below:

Black soot with faded prayer flags on a snowy high Himalayan pass. It is thought that up to half of glacial melt can be attributed to black soot (aka black carbon), caused by burning of fossil fuels which generate minuscule black soot particles in the atmosphere. Black soot absorbs the sun, speeding up glacial meltdown, while snow deflects the sun's rays. Cooking with cleaner cookstoves would result in far less black soot pollution. Cleaner cookstoves have been introduced in Nepal and other Himalayan areas, along with solar-powered cooking devices.

The Key to a Brighter Future?

Ladakh is building several solar plants in the desert with an output of 7.5 GW, equivalent to that of the largest dams in the world. Here is what His Holiness says about the solar revolution:

"Solar and wind energy are already the more economical sources of energy worldwide. So we don't need nuclear or coal-fired plants. We are at the beginning of a worldwide solar revolution. We must change our lifestyle and heavy reliance on old energy."

"One of my dreams, perhaps an impossible dream, is to harness the solar potential of places like the Sahara Desert and to use the power to run desalination plants. The sweet water thus produced could green the desert and produce food crops. It is a project that would have widespread benefits and would function on a scale that requires global cooperation."

Bhutan is the first nation in the world to foster all-organic crops. The next-door Indian state of Sikkim is also all-organic. That means no Genetically-Modified crops, and no use of toxic chemical herbicides or pesticides. Natural remedies like yak-urine are used instead.

Blue Poppy — *symbolic of the fragility of the high-altitude environment, flourishes in Bhutan. Often found growing at an altitude of over 4,000 metres, the blue poppy is the national flower of Bhutan. Life is harsh at altitude, and flora and fauna are uniquely adapted*

to this environment. The magnificent Blue Poppy was first discovered by a Western explorer in eastern Tibet, and its seeds were later cultivated in European gardens.

Above & Right:
Bhutan — *the greenest nation in Asia — HH Dalai Lama's vision to turn Tibet into the largest nature preserve on the planet has not come to pass. However, the nation of Bhutan has set aside 51% of its total land area for national parks, nature reserves and biological corridors. Bhutan is the first nation in the world to have achieved this 50%-plus ratio, envisaged by biologist E.O. Wilson as the Half-Earth Plan — the best way to save biodiversity. Forest cover in Bhutan is over 70% of land area — well ahead of any other nation in Asia.*

114

References & Resources

QUOTATIONS

The editor's primary source of quotations is a book regularly updated and published by the CTA, Dharamsala, India, titled: *His Holiness the 14th Dalai Lama on Environment: Collected Statements 1987-2018*. The seventh edition was edited by Tempa Gyaltsen Zamlha, Dechen Palmo and Tenzin Palden, researchers at the Environment & Development Desk, Tibet Policy Institute.

Other quotes are sourced from a range of interviews, speeches, messages and book introductions by His Holiness to mark special occasions and events such as Earth Day. When tied to specific context and timing, these quotes have been attributed directly on the relevant page. For instance, part of his December 1989 Nobel Acceptance Speech has been quoted. Short quotes have been culled from HH Dalai Lama's official Twitter account. Quoted several times are individual stanzas from a 30-stanza poem he wrote in Tibetan in 1993, then translated into English as: *The Sheltering Tree of Interdependence*.

Some longer quotes derive from books by His Holiness: *Ancient Wisdom, Modern World*; *The Universe in a Single Atom*; and *Beyond Religion: Ethics for the Whole World*.

Also consulted: *Our Only Home: A Climate Appeal to the World* (HH Dalai Lama and Franz Alt), *An Appeal to the World* (HH Dalai Lama/Franz Alt), and *A Call for Revolution* (HH Dalai Lama with Sofia Stril-Rever). Media sources tapped for quotations include Newsweek, TIME100, Time Magazine, The Guardian, the LA Times, and more. The editor has on occasion used video and audio recordings of His Holiness as source material.

UPDATED QUOTATIONS FROM HIS HOLINESS

www.dalailama.com gives lots of news and links.

HH Dalai Lama's official **Twitter account @DalaiLama** is a wonderful source of new quotations — as well as archived older ones. This has the advantage of presenting quotes in very compact format.

The official YouTube channel for HH Dalai Lama is a great resource for interviews, speeches, and so forth, but these could be difficult to transcribe. It is best to keep to official and verified sources for quotes from His Holiness.

HEARTFELT THANKS

Gratitude to His Holiness the Great 14th Dalai Lama, The Presence, the source of amazing inspiration and hope — a moral compass for so many in troubled times: an environmentalist with a life-long commitment to preserving Tibet's natural environment — which impacts the whole of Asia — and far beyond.

Special thanks to:
Tseten Samdup Chhoekyapa, at the Private Office of His Holiness, for his great patience and guidance.
Tempa Gyaltsen Zamlha and Dechen Palmo, at Tibet Policy Institute, who provided the spark and the framework for this book.

Tashi Norbu, Tibetan artist extraordinaire, whose beautiful thangka artwork is featured in several pages of this book. Gratitude to John Negru at Sumeru Books, who set the wheels in motion for getting this book into print.

My heartfelt thanks go to the photographers who generously allowed access to their finest photos. Without them, this work would never have seen the light of day: Tenzin Choejor, personal photographer for His Holiness, for his wonderful images, appearing on pages throughout this book.

Mountaineers Pat Morrow and Colin Monteath contributed sublime shots of snowcaps and glaciers, taking us where few mortals will ever set foot.

And thanks to Ian Baker, Manuel Bauer, Marcus Rhinelander, Brian Harris, Jonesy, Jay Monty, Matteo Pistono, Dick & Pip Smith, Mikael Lorin, Lobsang Wangyal and Abhishek Madhukar. Last but by no means least, I would like to thank Photographers Anonymous. Several key contributors wish to remain Incognito. High Five to the Incognitos — you know who you are!

ABOUT THE EDITOR

MICHAEL BUCKLEY is a Canadian photojournalist who has been involved in researching and writing about Tibet for over 35 years. He is author of *Meltdown in Tibet*, an exposé on China's reckless destruction of ecosystems from the highlands of Tibet to the deltas of Asia. He created a digital photo companion for this, titled *Tibet, Disrupted*, and is filmmaker for three short documentaries about environmental issues in Tibet. He is author of a children's book about Tibetan animals, titled *The Snow Leopard's New Friend*. Buckley has written a dozen books about the Himalayan and Southeast Asian regions, including *Tibet: the Bradt Travel Guide*. As a keen diver, he has a special interest in preserving the world's oceans, and is author of the digital photobook *Planet Ocean Blues*.

Author websites:
www.MeltdowninTibet.com
www.Himmies.com
FB.com/MeltdowninTibet

KEY PHOTO CONTRIBUTORS

TENZIN CHOEJOR is the Official photographer for His Holiness the Dalai Lama. He was born in Lhasa and came to India in 1987. He completed an MA in Mass Communications in 2005 at Madras Christian College, Chennai. Tenzin Choejor has taken most of the superb photos of His Holiness featured in this book.

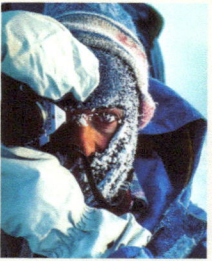

PAT MORROW first glimpsed the splendour of Tibet from the summit of Everest, near the culmination of the 1982 Canadian mountaineering expedition. He marvelled at the landscape, and, curious about the fate of its fabled people, set about visiting Tibet on six occasions, four of them being climbing expeditions. He went on to become the first to complete the climbers' version of the Seven Summits. As a photographer and filmmaker, he and his wife Baiba have spent the equivalent of three years trekking, climbing and travelling throughout the Tibetan diaspora in the Himalaya. They now channel their energy into volunteer efforts for the environmental organization Wildsight.
www.patmorrow.com

COLIN MONTEATH is a New Zealand based polar and mountain photographer who has been involved in 21 expeditions to various parts of the Himalaya, four of them in Tibet. He was a member of the 1984 Australian Everest expedition that climbed the white limbo route up the North Face. After trekking in from Nepal and making a circuit of Kailash, Colin almost reached the summit of Gurla Mandhata. He has also explored the Kangshung/Kharta watershed, east of Everest, and taken part in a New Zealand ski expedition that ventured into the Kangri Garpo Mountains in eastern Tibet, right on the Tibet-Burma border.
www.colinmonteath.nz

SELECTED READING

Our Only Home: A Climate Appeal to the World
HH Dalai Lama and Franz Alt. Bloomsbury, UK, November 2020. Based on extensive interviews with His Holiness by German journalist Franz Alt — about pressing environmental issues and the need for the world to come together to resolve them.

His Holiness the Fourteenth Dalai Lama: an Illustrated Biography. Tenzin Geyche Tethong (author). Interlink Pub Group, India, November, 2020.
This comprehensive tome contains over 400 rare photos and documents about the spiritual icon.

Moral Ground: Ethical Action for a Planet in Peril
Kathleen Dean Moore and Michael P. Nelson (editors). Trinity University Press, Texas, 2010. This hefty volume sets out to answer the question: 'Do we have a moral obligation to take action to protect the future of a planet in peril?' HH Dalai Lama is among those to provide answers.

SHORT FILMS

feedbackloopsclimate.com
Climate Emergency: Feedback Loops
Short films on major climate issues, narrated by Richard Gere. Presented by the Mind & Life Institute, which was co-founded by HH Dalai Lama to bring science and contemplative wisdom together to better understand the mind and create positive change in the world.

COPYRIGHT & CREDITS

THIS FRAGILE PLANET
His Holiness the Dalai Lama on Environment
First Sumeru Books edition 2021

Copyright © Gaden Phodrang Foundation of the Dalai Lama /Michael Buckley All Rights Reserved

ISBN: 978-1-896559-73-5

Editing and compilation: Michael Buckley
Book design: Stephanie Bonheur
Proofreader: Riina Tamm
Photos: contributed by more than a dozen photographers.

A modified ebook version of this book is available on Apple Books and other platforms, published by ThunderHorse Media.

The Sumeru Press Inc.
sumeru-books.com

འཇིག་རྟེན་སྐྱེ་བའི་འཇམ་སྦྱིན།

Library and Archives Canada Cataloguing in Publication

Title: This fragile planet : His Holiness the Dalai Lama on environment / photography & text compiled & edited by Michael Buckley.
Names: Bstan-'dzin-rgya-mtsho, Dalai Lama XIV, 1935- author. | Buckley, Michael, 1950- editor.
Description: First Sumeru Books edition.
Identifiers: Canadiana 20210213515 | ISBN 9781896559735 (softcover)
Subjects: LCSH: Bstan-'dzin-rgya-mtsho, Dalai Lama XIV, 1935-—Quotations.
  | LCSH: Human ecology— Religious aspects—Buddhism—Quotations, maxims, etc.
  | LCSH: Environmental protection—Religious aspects—Buddhism—Quotations, maxims, etc.
  | LCSH: Buddhism—Doctrines. | LCGFT: Quotations.
Classification: LCC BQ4570.E23 B78 2021 | DDC 294.3/377—dc23

www.ingramcontent.com/pod-product-compliance
Lightning Source LLC
Chambersburg PA
CBHW041646220426

43665CB00005B/71